NATIONALISM IN HINDU CULTURE

NATIONALISM IN HINDU CULTURE

RADHAKUMUD MOOKERJI

GYAN

Published by

Gyan Publishing House
5, Ansari Road
Daryaganj, New Delhi-110002
Phone: 011-47034999, 9811692060
E-mail: books@gyanbooks.com

Distribution Network
gyanbooks.com
India, USA, Canada, UK, Australia, France

ISBN : 978-81-212-9476-8 (PB)
First Published, 1921

2nd Impression 2023

Printed at: Gyan Press, Delhi.

NATIONALISM IN HINDU CULTURE
Author: RADHAKUMUD MOOKERJI

Mysore University Extension Lectures, 1920

NATIONALISM IN HINDU CULTURE

NATIONALISM IN HINDU CULTURE

BY

RADHAKUMUDa MOOKERJI

M.A., PH.D., PREMCHAND ROYCHAND SCHOLAR (CALCUTTA UNIVERSITY), VIDYAVAIBHAVA PROFESSOR OF HISTORY, MYSORE UNIVERSITY

AUTHOR OF
"A HISTORY OF INDIAN SHIPPING," "THE FUNDAMENTAL UNITY OF INDIA," "LOCAL GOVERNMENT IN ANCIENT INDIA," ETC.

1921

PREFACE

The present work consists of Extension Lectures delivered under the auspices of the Mysore University. I have developed in them some of the ideas broached in one of my earlier works, *The Fundamental Unity of India* (Longmans, London, 1914), being encouraged to do so by their endorsement by that critical historian, the late Dr Vincent A. Smith (*vide* his *Oxford History of India*, p. xiii), as well as by the interest taken in them by some esteemed friends and publicists. The purpose of the Lectures accounts for their limitations as regards their matter and manner. The style is popular, and at times polemic and iterative; for, in delivering such lectures, "one ought," as Lord Haldane well points out, "to watch one's audience, to follow the working of its mind, and to mould one's discourse accordingly" (*Gifford Lectures*, p. viii). Similarly, the treatment does not aim at a scholarly completeness in respect of the evidence and arguments adduced. The Lectures first appeared as they were delivered, in the *Commonweal*, from which they are reprinted by the kind permission of Mrs Annie Besant, to whom my best thanks are due for undertaking this publication.

The Lectures, while utilising well-known sources and materials, claim originality as regards the particular use made of them and the standpoint from which they have been viewed. They develop a common theme dealing with the *bases* of Nationalism in Ancient India. They do not, however, deal with the *superstructure* built upon these bases, with the constitution and composition of that particular type of polity which the Hindu principles and ideals of Nationalism developed in India. The study of that multiform polity, as represented and embodied in diverse types of group-life, of corporations and communal institutions formed on all possible principles of association, functional, local, or voluntary, requires a comprehensive and special treatment, such as that attempted in my monograph, *Local Government in Ancient India* (Clarendon Press, Oxford, 2nd ed., 1920), to which the reader is accordingly referred. A general indication, however, of the full content of Ancient Indian Nationalism, together with its institutional embodiments, is given in the concluding chapter by way of stimulating further interest in the subject.

My thanks are due to Messrs Longmans, Green & Co., London, for permission to reproduce some passages from my earlier work, which are indicated within quotation marks.

The transliteration of Samskrit words is not given, as being unsuited to a popular work of this character.

CONTENTS

CHAP.		PAGE
I.	PRELIMINARY—PRACTICAL SIDE OF HINDU CULTURE	1
2.	PATRIOTISM IN SAMSKRIT LITERATURE .	9
3.	THE HINDU CONCEPTION OF PATRIOTISM .	17
4.	THE HINDU INSTITUTION OF PILGRIMAGE AND ITS SIGNIFICANCE	33
5.	PILGRIMAGE AS FOSTERING PATRIOTISM AND NATIONALISM IN ANCIENT INDIA .	39
6.	NATIONALISM IN SAMSKRIT LITERATURE .	46
7.	THE NATIONALISM OF HINDU SECTS . .	57
8.	NATIONALISM AS A HINDU POLITICAL IDEAL	68
9.	SAMSKRIT LITERATURE AND ITS BEARING ON NATIONAL LIFE	76
10.	THE CULTURAL EQUIPMENT OF SAMSKRIT LITERATURE	89
11.	CONCLUSION	96

NATIONALISM IN HINDU CULTURE

PRELIMINARY

THERE is a widespread misconception that the Hindus have never been a practical people, that while they have succeeded so signally in the sphere of speculation they have failed equally in the sphere of action. Thus ancient Hindu culture and civilisation in this view present a development which was merely one-sided instead of being an harmonious whole.

Of course, no student of early Indian history can doubt or deny the marked triumphs and achievements of the Hindu genius in the domain of mental, moral, and spiritual progress. None can be blind to the vast mass of literature which conveys to lettered humanity conceptions about laws and customs, manners and morals, cults and creeds, betokening a culture as wide as deep and a social development of a most advanced type. The discovery of Samskrit by the West has led the way to a far more important discovery of the proper place of Hindu thought in the culture-history of the world. Vague and conflicting notions about the mere external accidents and superficial aspects of Hindu life have now yielded their place to a genuine, systematic, and scientific appreciation of Hindu philosophical and religious systems, and a due recognition is at last made of the immense value of the special contributions made to the progress of humanity as a whole by the Hindu people.

It is, in a word, to her philosophy that India at present owes the respect of the world. That, however, points to mere intellectual and spiritual activity and progress, and is no argument for success in the sphere of action. The appreciation of Hindu culture has, therefore, naturally confined itself to its mental and moral aspects, to the neglect of the material and practical; and the belief has gained ground that Hindu genius is almost exclusively speculative and not at all practical.

This belief, however, cannot be well founded. The history of civilisation shows that even mental and moral development rests on a material basis, and presupposes economic activity and progress. The narrow view of Hindu culture which sees in it the mere workings of metaphysical intellect and speculative genius has to be corrected by a consideration of its practical aspects. Our study of ancient Hindu culture-history has hitherto mostly confined itself indeed to its subjective aspects, to the records it presents of mental, moral, and spiritual development, and has not adequately attended to its objective or positive aspects—the records of material progress and secular achievements. What is, therefore, wanted is a systematic study of the activities and achievements of the ancient Hindus in the secular sphere, in the realm of action, so that we may be enabled to arrive at a fuller and a more proper estimate of their culture and civilisation which were capable of producing not merely poets and prophets, saints and seers, monks and mendicants, men of thought and men of letters, but also men of action and men of affairs, politicians and practical administrators, heroes and warriors, kings and emperors, statesmen and diplomats. Hindu India produced and is famous not merely for immortal literature, unique in its vastness, variety and longevity, but also for polities and administrations which culminated in the great empires of the Mauryas and Guptas, empires that sometimes controlled a continent stretching from Afghanistan to Mysore. Chanakya and Chandragupta, Asoka and Samudragupta, Charaka and Sushruta, Aryabhatta and Varahamihira,

Nagarjuna and Palakapya are names as famous in Indian history as Vasishtha and Visvamitra, Valmiki and Vyasa, Kapila and Kanada, Buddha and Mahavira, Panini and Kalidasa. Indeed, our studies in Hindu literature should now address themselves to its practical aspects rather than to the philosophical, should relate themselves to the results of Hindu thought as directed to the phenomena and processes of the world without, rather than to the world within, so that a comprehensive account may be given of the natural philosophy which is embedded in the principal systems of Hindu thought. That such studies will be fruitful goes without saying. We already know some of their results. We already know something of the great achievements of the ancient Hindus in such scientific and practical subjects as medicine and surgery, applied chemistry and pharmacy, or in the many arts of civilised life, such as architecture, sculpture, painting, metallurgy, and dyeing, or in the numerous handicrafts which established and maintained for a long time the dominance of India in the ancient commercial world. We also know how India attained, and long maintained, a pre-eminent position in the ancient commercial world, which is another proof of the practical genius of her people. But it is not equally known that India owed that proud position to her important discoveries in applied chemistry, her inimitable skill in handicrafts, which enabled her to produce those manufactures and articles of luxury of which India enjoyed a monopoly in the ancient commercial world, having the Roman Empire as her principal customer. Nor is it sufficiently known that her commercial supremacy was but the handmaid of her national marine. This was true of every country in the world in olden days, and it would have been strange if it had not been true of India too. It is an historical commonplace and quite stands to reason that no commerce could spring up, much less thrive, in early times unless it were fed by a national shipping. Students of Indian history have yet to learn the great part played by Indian shipping in carrying Indian art and culture across the seas to distant lands together with her material products. At the foundation of a greater India there lay the Indian Marine. It was the maritime activity of the Hindus which offered scope to their other activities in foreign lands and multiplied centres of Hindu influence beyond the limits of Hindu India.

The history of Indian maritime activity, though a forgotten chapter of Indian history, has great value as demonstrating the practical capacities of the Hindu genius in days of yore. Navigation, and especially ocean navigation, is one of the most difficult arts, and the pursuit of that art in ages long before the application of steam to locomotion must have multiplied its difficulties, which could only have been met by a corresponding amount of daring and enterprise, skill and resourcefulness. To show how far the pursuit of that art was successful, the two following testimonies among others may be quoted:

A French writer, F. B. Solvyns, writes thus in his *Les Hindous* (1811):

> "In ancient times the Indians excelled in the art of constructing vessels, and the present Hindus can, in this respect, still offer models to Europe, so much so that the English, attentive to everything which relates to naval architecture, have borrowed from the Hindus many improvements which they have adapted with success to their own shipping. The Indian vessels unite elegance and utility, and are models of patience and fine workmanship."

Similarly that distinguished Englishman, Sir John Malcolm, thus writes in the first volume of the *Journal of the Royal Asiatic Society*, London:

> "Indian vessels are so admirably adapted to the purposes for which they are required that, notwithstanding their superior science, Europeans were unable, during an intercourse

> with India for two centuries, to suggest or to bring into successful practice one improvement."

The fact of the matter is that the theory has to be abandoned which associates with ancient India an exclusive progress in the domain of barren philosophy and spiritual speculation and no achievements in the practical domain of economic activity, for the evidence of sober, trustworthy history proves beyond doubt that ancient India was as great in action as in thought. There is evidence to show that for fully a thousand years, from Pliny to Tavernier, she commanded the markets of the East as well as the West, and achieved an easy and long-continued predominance in the ancient commercial world by virtue of her remarkable progress in the production of various manufactures—which was again due to her progress in her handicrafts, in applied chemistry, and in metallurgy, to which the ancient world owed its Damascus blades. The truth is that India was able to hold her own in the ancient civilised world in every department of human activity, mental or material, moral or physical, secular or spiritual. The various ancient foreign writers on India are unanimous in their testimony regarding the remarkable economic progress and development of the country in the days of her Hindu rule—the

Greek writers like Megasthenes and the Chinese writers like Fa-Hien, Hiuen Tsang, and I-Tsing. This harmonious development in both the two fields of thought and action, of spiritual and material progress, is also reflected in the national Samskrit literature of the country, for the literature of a country always tells its life. A close examination of the vast Samskrit literature will not fail to discover its remarkable richness in point of works bearing on the manifold departments of the economic life of the country.

PATRIOTISM IN SAMSKRIT LITERATURE

THE harmonious development of ancient India in the manifold domains of national life is proved not merely by the testimony of history but also by that of her national literature. A close examination of Samskrit literature will easily reveal the truth that it contains within itself all the elements that are needed to develop the different interests of national life, mental or moral, spiritual and practical. Just as this material mother-country of ours, this vast Indian continent stretching from Kashmir to Cape Comorin, is endowed by nature with magnificent physical potentialities and resources which, if properly developed, are calculated to make her economically self-sufficient and independent, similarly this vast Samskrit literature is extraordinarily rich in all those mental and moral, religious and spiritual elements and resources which are necessary for the cultural life and independence of a nation, and were once found adequate enough to build up the culture and civilisation of ancient

India. In fact, all that is needed for the wholesome development of national life was being amply supplied by the principal medium and vehicle of the culture of the country in ancient times. It is too often assumed that, like Hindu civilisation, Samskrit literature represents only a one-sided development, being composed exclusively of only one type of literature and characterised by only one type of thought, viz. the religious and spiritual. It is too often assumed that Samskrit literature is always and exclusively preoccupied with the things of the other world, the interests of the hereafter and not with those of this world or the practical interests of the present time and the life on earth. It is, therefore, assumed that Samskrit literature is potentially and actually incapable of ministering in any way and in the slightest degree to the manifold and novel requirements of modern life under the conditions of present-day progress. For instance, the modern world is characterised by the growth of nationalism, the spirit of patriotism or love of one's mother-country as the preliminary stage in the progress of the various peoples of the world towards cosmopolitanism, internationalism, a sense of universal brotherhood, of the essential unity of mankind, towards world-federation or the parliament of man. Internationalism indeed presupposes a keen nationalism, a sensitive spirit of patriotism, which will lead the individual to realise a larger unity in that group of individuals which, along with him, make up his country commanding the service and homage of all her sons as children of a common soil. But it is asked, How far is Samskrit literature capable of supplying the food that is necessary to nourish this elementary spirit of patriotism? The doubt is always expressed that there are hardly any passages in Samskrit literature which give expression to the sentiments which are so warmly expressed, for example, in those famous lines of Scott:

> "Breathes there the man, with soul so dead,
> Who never to himself hath said,
> This is my own, my native land!"

It is always taken for granted that this love for the mere material aspect of the country, this devotion and attachment to the mere place or soil, the land of one's birth, is something quite foreign to the very spirit of Samskrit literature, is something quite unworthy of its predominantly philosophical and spiritual preoccupations and tendencies; for it is too much engrossed with heaven and the hereafter to have any thought left for the sordid interests of the material life on the earth below. This is, indeed, a line of thought and criticism applied to Samskrit literature which is naturally suggested by the extraordinary richness, vastness, and variety of the philosophical and religious aspects of Samskrit literature, the glare of which blinds us to its other aspects. It is high time that an attempt should be made to make a juster appreciation of the completeness of the cultural equipment that Samskrit literature affords, ministering as it did, in the olden days of Hindu India, to all the manifold interests of national life, material and moral, secular and spiritual. Indeed it may be assumed on mere *a priori* grounds that just as India was economically and politically an independent unit capable of asserting her rightful place in the ancient international world, she was also equally self-sufficient and independent in point of her cultural life and development; that her own languages and literatures were quite adequate for purposes of supplying her with all that moral and spiritual food which was necessary for the very development of her national life.

But the truth of this argument is amply borne out by facts. A critical study of Samskrit literature will be able to discover many passages bearing on the widespread consciousness of a keen sense of patriotism. Indeed, an intense passion for the fatherland utters itself throughout Samskrit literature. The very first factor of nation-building being an absorbing passion for the place of one's birth, it is no wonder that Samskrit literature should contribute towards its growth, as it had contributed towards the growth of the other interests of a healthy national life. Thoughout the vast range of Samskrit literature one can gather various references to this particular feeling, and we may in this connection refer to the more typical of them. For instance, in the Vedic literature we have a most remarkable passage in the *Atharvaveda* called the Prithivi Sukta, which is a string of about sixty-three impassioned hymns to the motherland. Praises are sung of the mother-country as the land girt by the sea and fertilised by the rivers that pour down their bounty in streams of plenty, the land of hills and snowy mountains and forests giving protection to her sons "unharassed, unsmitten, and unwounded"; the all-producing mother of herbs maintained by the auspicious and the pleasant; the land where our forefathers lived and worked, where the Asuras succumbed to the might of the Devas; the land of agriculture, of kine, of horses, of birds, of elephants; the land "bearing in many places people of different speech, of diverse customs according to their homes, yet yielding a thousand streams of property like a steady, unresisting milch-cow." The last passage is indeed highly significant for the unique note it strikes—remarkable for that age—showing a seer's grasp of the fundamental conditions of nation-building in this land of " many peoples of different speech and diverse customs." And yet this very diversity is recognised in a supremely patriotic spirit as a source of national strength, of that richer and fuller unity in which all diversities lose themselves with their several contributions towards the development of a common life, even as "a thousand steams" merge themselves in the sea. One verse gives expression to the following impassioned sentiment :

> "What many roads thou hast for people to go upon, a track for the chariot and for the going of the cart—that road free from enemies, free from robbers."

Another refers to the political growth of the times in these appreciative words :

> "What villages, what forests, what assemblies are upon thee ;
>
> "What hosts, gatherings—in them we may speak what is pleasant to thee"

—a reference to the *sabhas* and *samitis* of Vedic India in which the gift of eloquence in debates was regarded as a precious possession. And in the last passage runs the following noble prayer:

> "O Mother Earth, do thou kindly set me down, well-established;
> "In concord with the heaven, O Sage, do thou set me in fortune, in prosperity"

—a characteristic Hindu prayer "true to the kindred points of Heaven and Home."

But this expression of an intense feeling for the fatherland is not the solitary peculiarity of the Vedic literature alone, for later Samskrit literature abounds in expressions of the same feeling. Who does not know the most familiar passage of Manu in which he defines the motherland in his grateful appreciation of the untold blessings and benefits derived from her as the country fashioned by the very hands of the Gods. The same sentiment receives a culminating expression in a famous passage in the *Vishnupurana*, where Bharatavarsha is extolled "as the best of all countries," where "it is only after many thousand births, and the aggregation of much merit that living beings are sometimes born as men,"—about which the Gods themselves exclaimed: "Happy are those who are born even from the condition of Gods as men in Bharatavarsha, as that is the way to the pleasures of Paradise, or the greater blessing of final liberation. Happy are they who, consigning all the unheeded rewards to the supreme and eternal Vishnu, obtain existence in that land of works as their path to Him. We know not when the acts that have attained us heaven shall have been fully recompensed, where we shall renew corporeal confinement, but we know that those men are fortunate who are born with perfect faculties in Bharatavarsha." There cannot be found in any other literature expressions of a more fervent patriotism than that which utters itself in these passages in which the country is applauded as being the creation of divine architects, as being a habitation worthy of the Gods themselves, as a veritable heaven on earth. This deification of the motherland and attribution to her of a divine making, is as characteristic of Samskrit literature as it is unusual to the spirit of the literatures of other countries. We may finally recall in this connection the great utterance :

> "JANANI JANMABHUMISCHA SWARGADAPI GARIYASI. 'The Mother and Motherland are higher than heaven itself.'"

HINDU CONCEPTION OF PATRIOTISM

SAMSKRIT literature is abounding in patriotic passages, but the most remarkable of them is undoubtedly that comprised by the Prithivi Sukta of the *Atharvaveda* just cited. The passage is unique in the entire range of that vast literature, in the width of vision it exhibits, the intensity of its patriotic fervour, and the depth of its penetrating analysis, unfolding under the inspiration of a truly spiritual power of insight the manifold gifts and blessings with which nature has endowed the land we live in. It is scarcely possible for any modern writer on economics to improve upon the treatment given in this sacred work of the well-worn familiar topic discussed in the various text-books of Indian economics, viz. the influence of the physical environment of India upon the development of her economic life. The poet of the *Atharvaveda* deals with that topic in a most masterly and, at the same time, most impassioned manner. He refers by turns to all the precious free gifts which nature has so lavishly bestowed upon our fatherland, gifts which distinguished India from most of the countries of the world in their abundance, variety, and potentialities, the natural endowments which definitely promise India the rare career and destiny of an economic self-sufficiency and independence. The account in the *Atharvaveda* of the wealth of India derived from natural sources deserves and will repay our examination. We need not refer in this connection to each and all of the sixty-three impassioned verses which make up that account. It will suffice for our purpose if we confine ourselves to the few typical ones, each of which reveals one particular aspect of that abundant natural endowment of our country with which, as her preliminary capital, she has been started on her economic career.

The first feature noted by the *Atharvaveda* poet is the primary one of the physical, territorial extent of the country, which is the basis of all life. The very expansion of the people, the growth of their numbers, and the spread of their civilisation depend upon that primary gift of a wide stretch of territory, in point of which India is one of the most fortunate and best-endowed countries of the world; and so this preliminary formative factor of her national life is expressed in the prayer :

> "Let the country make for us wide room ; let the country be spread out for us, be prosperous for us,
>
> "On whom our forefathers formerly spread themselves upon the brown, black, red, all-formed fixed soil the inhabitants of which stand, unharassed, unsmitten, and unwounded."

The value of this primal gift of nature is thus expressed in the following prayer inspired by an overflowing religious emotion :

> "When yonder, O Divine One, spreading thyself forward, thou didst expand in greatness, then entered into thee well-being ; thou didst make fit the four directions ; thou art the scatterer of people."

There is next a reference to the physical configuration, the division of the land surface into plains and hills.

Thirdly, there are repeated appreciative references to the great part played in the economic development of the country by its rivers. The reference of the *Atharvaveda* to these beneficent natural agencies is indeed an echo of the earlier passage of the *Rigveda* known as the "River Hymn," in which are mentioned the various rivers of the Punjab, these perennial streams of plenty and good to which the country owes so much, which were at once the highways of commerce and culture alike, and are naturally deified by a grateful imagination and receive the nation's worship and homage.

> "O ye Ganga, Yamuna, Saraswati, Satadru, and Parusni, receive ye my prayers. O ye Marutbridha joined by the Asikni, Vitasta, and Arjikiya joined by the Sushoma, hear ye my prayers."

Here patriotism itself is elevated and refined into religion. The contemplation of the profound economic significance of those natural agencies has led the poet's mind from nature up to nature's God. To think of the mother-country, to adore her as the visible giver of all good becomes a religious duty; the fatherland is allotted its rightful place in the nation's daily prayers, the fatherland of which the most important manifestation is constituted by the river systems. The *Atharvaveda* takes up this earlier note of the *Rigveda* and devotes to the same theme quite a number of verses:

> "On whom the circulating waters flow the same, day and night, without failure—let that land of many streams yield us milk; then let her sprinkle us with splendour.
>
> "Let cleansed waters flow for our body."

Along with the rivers, the hills and forests which constitute the other important elements of national wealth receive a due reference.

> "Let thy hills and snowy mountains, let thy forest land be pleasant. Rock is this soil, stone, dust; this soil is held together; to that soil have I paid homage.
>
> "On whom stand always fixed the trees, the forest trees, the all-supporting soil that is held together do we address."

Along with forests there is a reference to the wild animals inhabiting them:

> "What forest animals of thine, wild beasts set in the woods, lions, tigers, go about man eating—the jackal, the wolf, do thou force from us away here.
>
> "What odour of thine in horses, in wild animals and in elephants."

And also to serpents:

> "What stinging, harsh-biting serpent of thine lies in secret, winter-harmed, torpid; whatever worm becoming lively stirs in the early rainy season—let that, crawling, not crawl upon us; be thou gracious to us with that which is propitious to us."

Also to birds:

> "Two-footed winged ones, swans, eagles, hawks, birds."

There are also a few impassioned references to the agricultural wealth of the country, which is one of the best of nature's gifts to India :

> "On whom food, ploughings, came into being ;
> "The all-producing mother of herbs on whom is food, rice, and barley."

Nor is the wealth of the country that is hidden in the bowels of her soil forgotten :

> "Bearing treasure and gold in many places hiddenly, let the earth give me jewel, gold."

Nor also is the "atmospheric income" enjoyed by the country omitted :

> "Both heaven and earth and atmosphere have given me this expanse ; fire, sun, waters, and all the Gods have together given me wisdom.
> "Let thy hot season, rainy season, autumn, winter, cool season, spring—let thine arranged seasons, years, let day and night, yield benefit to us."

We may note the significance of the "arranged seasons" of India and the "benefits" they naturally confer upon her economic life in general and agriculture in particular.

There is also a passing reference to the live stock, the domesticated animals necessary to an agricultural civilisation. One verse addresses a prayer to the mother-country "as the station of kine and horses."

Another runs thus :

> "Let us be set among kine, also in inexhaustibleness."

The motherland is also extolled for her riches in human kind and her stock of artificial wealth which represents man's gifts to her as distinguished from Nature's. There is first a reference to the wealth of the country in heroes and heroism :

> "On whom the people of old formerly spread themselves ; on whom the Gods overcame the Asuras."

Herein is a well-deserved and significant reference to the undaunted spirit of the early pioneers of the Indo-Aryan civilisation who were propagating it all over India through inevitable and hard struggles and conflicts with the indigenous civilisations and peoples. She is extolled as the land of Vedic sacrifices "on which are set up the sacrificial posts erect and bright," "where men give to the Gods the sacrifices, the oblation duly prepared."

One verse appreciates the character of the inhabitants thus :

> "What odour of thine in human beings ; in women, in men, what portion, pleasure."

Another repeats the previous note :

> "On whom are the seat and oblation hall ; on whom the sacrificial post is planted ; on whom the Brahmanas praise with verses, with the chant, knowing the sacrificial formulæ ; on whom are joined the priests."

The country is also extolled in a number of verses as giving protection to her sons.

> "Whose are the God-made strongholds ;
>
> "Let the land push forth our rivals, let her make us free from rivals ;
>
> "Let not the waylayers find us ; keep very far off the deadly weapon ;
>
> "Let no one soever hate us ; whoso shall hate us, whoso shall fight us, whoso vex us with mind, who with deadly weapon—him do thou put in our power ;
>
> "She whom the Gods sleepless defend all the time without failure."

There is again a surprising reference (already cited) to the wealth of the country in the means and facilities of commercial intercourse :

> "What many roads thou hast for people to go upon, a track for the chariot, and for the going of the cart, by which men of both kinds, excellent and evil, go about—that road free from enemies, free from robbers may we conquer ; be thou gracious to us with that which is propitious."

The entire civilisation of the country is summed up again in the following remarkable verse :

> "What villages, what forests, what assemblies are upon thee, what hosts, gatherings—in them may we speak what is pleasing to thee."

Herein is an unmistakable reference to the progress of settled life among the Vedic Indians, which paved the way for considerable political development as represented in institutions or assemblies, called in the original *Sabhas* and *Samitis*, and also occasional public meetings and conferences, through which the public life and spirit of the community expressed themselves. Eloquence in assemblies and meetings, especially the eloquence that is pleasant to the audience, is prized as a most desirable accomplishment. This is reaffirmed in another verse :

> "What I speak, rich in honey I speak it ; what I view, that they win me ; brilliant am I, possessed of swiftness ; I smite down others that are violent."

One of the most valuable elements of national wealth is undoubtedly that which accrues from a free and well-ordered State, comprising civil and military security and the manifold blessings of life under free institutions, and accordingly, the freedom of life, which the citizens of the country enjoyed in the Vedic period, forms an additional link in the chain of numerous blessings which binds them in indissoluble ties of gratitude to their motherland, and hence this praise of "assemblies," "hosts" and "gatherings" in this remarkable prayer.

Lastly, love of the country in the following passage already referred to is made, in a strictly Hindu way, properly subordinated to the higher duty towards God, to spiritual laws, to religious ideals :

> "O Mother Earth, do thou kindly set me down well-established ;
>
> "In concord with the heaven, O Sage, do thou set me in fortune, in prosperity."

Too much emphasis on patriotism or nationalism has the risk of leading the mind towards a craving for material possessions, towards things of this world, away from the things of the spirit. Nationalism has been recently defined by the great Indian poet, Sir Rabindranath Tagore, as being in essence a "gregariousness of gluttony." Patriotism may easily degenerate into a demand for the exclusive enjoyment of the good things of the earth *in* which the share of others is forcibly excluded. Hence worldly prosperity is not to be desired in the above-quoted prayer in violation of the laws of heaven. Patriotism must not be allowed to degenerate into materialism.

We thus see that the patriotism to which the *Atharvaveda* gives expression is not of the nature of a mere sickly sentimentalism or the vapourings of an overheated imagination, but is of the nature of that robust and practical patriotism which is broad based upon a reasoned appreciation and analysis of the manifold contributions made to our economic life and progress by the country as representing the physical environment thereof. It is a keen realisation of the immense debt of endless gratitude that has inspired the whole prayer embodying a fairly critical and scientific analysis of the various factors moulding the economic life of the country. The different items and constituents of national wealth as determined by modern economic writers are all mentioned in this ancient text. The free gifts of Nature in the three planes constituting what is *above* the surface of the earth, what is *below* it, and what is *on* it—all these are methodically mentioned. The country is worshipped for her gifts of the treasures of agricultural wealth, the richness of her botanical and zoological wealth, the vegetable and animal products, her splendid live stock, as also her mineral wealth ; she is duly appreciated for the atmospheric wealth she brings, the congenial character of her climates, her seasons—nay, her very days and nights; and, lastly, she is remarkable for her *human* wealth, her heroic sons that have civilised the whole continent, assimilating the aboriginal elements, established peace and order, given that protection which made political progress possible, the development of free institutions, a free public life expressing itself in meetings of assemblies and appreciation of eloquence in debate—gifts which made the country so eminently habitable and so warmly loved by her children in ancient times.

The feeling for the fatherland, far from being the peculiarity and solitary characteristic of Vedic literature, receives a continued expression throughout the later literature. We find it even deepening and gaining in volume. The most famous of our law books, viz. *Manusmriti*, in spite of its predominant preoccupation with dry social regulations and restrictions and prosaic problems of law, rises to a great height of emotional outburst in the passage in which it defines the limits of the country called Brahmavarta, which is described as "the land created by the gods." The conception of this remarkable definition is certainly worthy of that of the English poet who burst out in the following appreciative exclamation :

"England, with all thy faults, I love thee still."

But perhaps the Hindu law book reaches the high-water mark of passionate fondness for the country as a mere material entity, for the poet behind the law-giver, with his eyes in a fine frenzy rolling, cannot think of a more adequate and fitting characterisation of his country than the attribution of her making to the very hands of the gods—the country that showers upon her sons the felicities of heaven. It should, however, be remembered that this reverential attitude towards the country is not to be regarded as being temporarily induced by a passing fit of poetical exaggeration ; it was not by any means a happy hit of the moment, or the inconstant mood of a solitary admirer, author, or poet. The *Manusmriti* does not give expression to individual views, opinions, and sentiments, but to those of the nation. Manu is a mirror of the age, reflecting the manners, customs, and opinions of the entire nation. The attitude he expresses in the passage represents the settled habit of thought of the entire nation, the formed faith of the people. It represents a definite reality, a living truth, an essential article of the people's creed and faith, an abiding principle of Hinduism on which its believers sincerely act. The Hindus in their heart of hearts believe that theirs is a chosen land, where men must be born to be worthy of final salvation. This represents the national belief on the subject, and the passage of Manu is not a mere poetical metaphor but an expression of a widespread and deeply felt national sentiment all over the country. The country is universally regarded by her children as more sacred than heaven itself, and worthy of the habitation of the gods themselves.

What Manu has only briefly and in a passing fashion expressed, is elaborated with full details by another sacred and famous Samskrit text, the *Vishnupurana*, which is a popular book meant for the masses for their education in the sacred lore. There it is frankly stated that birth in this land is the final felicity rewarding the spiritual merit accumulated through a thousand lives, for it is held that a life in this holy land has a better chance of putting an end to the continuous revolution of the wheel of births and deaths in which human beings are caught up. It is even recognised that those who were born in this land have a prospect of attaining to a greater height of self-development than that attained by the gods themselves, viz. "the greater blessing of Final Liberation." Accordingly, the gods themselves are made to express their hearts' desire that, after the natural termination of their period of sojourn in heaven, they should be blessed with the good fortune of renewing their corporeal confinement in Bharatavarsha, for here men have the unique good fortune of realising religious truths through the inherent difficulties of mortal existence in a land which affords the most congenial environment for the practice of spiritual meditations leading to unlimited self-development. The sentiment of the *Vishnupurana* is also repeated on similar lines in another of our most popular religious books, viz. the *Bhagavatapurana*. All these are not primarily poetical works, but the sacred and serious literature of the people, in which are fixed the doctrines of their faith, the articles of their creed, the cherished principles of their abiding religious beliefs and convictions. The attitude towards the country that they exhibit, the view-point that they hold forth, the peculiar outlook they represent, are matters of permanent faith with the people, who were thus trained by their own Sastras in habits of paying homage to their native country, which they should worship and serve in the same way and in the same spirit in which they worship and serve their own deities. There is no distinction tolerated here between the material country, the giver of all good, the supporter and sustainer of life itself, the prime cause of all progress, and the heaven or god attained through such life and such progress.

Patriotism has thus to be cultivated as a religious emotion necessary for religious progress and not to be confined in its range within the limited horizon of a mere concern for the material interests of the country. The place of birth is sincerely regarded as a most important factor of emancipation itself. It is doubtful whether in any other literature of the world we can find similar expressions of patriotism under which the solid material earth becomes transfigured and deified into a spiritual ideal claiming the worship of the heart, for these expressions are characteristic of the Hindu mind, which alone can think of according to the motherland an honoured place among the gods of their elaborate pantheon. Patriotism itself is thus Indianised, receiving a distinctive expression of its own under the peculiar idealising and spiritualising process of Hindu thought.

THE HINDU INSTITUTION OF PILGRIMAGE AND ITS SIGNIFICANCE

The institution of pilgrimage is one of the distinguishing characteristics of ancient Hindu civilisation and culture. In no other country of the world do we find such an elaborate network of shrines and sacred places as has been spread over this vast mother-country of ours by the religious enthusiasm of the people which has sought to adore the country in that particular manner. Indeed, if we carefully examine the origin of this peculiar institution that has made its influence felt throughout the country in all its parts and in all the ages of its history, we shall be bound to conclude that it is but one of the modes in which the patriotism of the Hindu has chosen to express itself. It goes without saying that the institution of pilgrimage is ultimately an expression of love for the motherland, one of the characteristic Hindu modes of worship of the country. The feeling for the fatherland, in the intensity of its fervour, has sought to create thousands of holy places all over the country so that every part thereof may be held sacred and worthy of worship. The patriot prostrates himself in worship at myriads of holy places into which the immensity of the sacred body of the motherland has been conveniently divided up for the individual realisation by finite minds of her transcendental sanctity. This undoubtedly indicates the formative factor behind this extraordinarily Indian institution, which is not to be found elsewhere in the world.

It should also be noted that behind the purely religious merit and spiritual benefits associated with the institution, there is the underlying factor of the passion for place, the appreciation of geographical significance, and the admiration of art. Benares in the north, and Kanchi in the south, are loved and visited, not only because they have been sanctified by religious men and movements, by associations of saints and scholars, but also because they are themselves beautiful places, which are a "a joy for ever," because they are cathedral cities, rich in architecture and works of art. In the same way the sheer beauty of the sea has had much to do with the growth of Puri or Jagannath as one of the holiest places of India, together with perhaps the other historical factor of the cosmopolitanism of the place as the port through which long flowed the eastern trade of India. Similarly, Allahabad becomes inevitably the prince of holy places for its enviable situation at the confluence of two mighty rivers mingling their waters. The perennial beauty of the Himalayas again has immortally impressed itself upon the national mind of India and has made them the chosen abode of contemplation and piety, whither flow perpetual streams of pilgrims. Indeed, the Hindu's pilgrimages are always to the glacier-clad mountains, the palm-clad seashore, or ocean isle, or the almost impenetrable depths of hill and wood where the tread of man has scarcely been heard, and nature has been left free to exercise undisturbed her spiritualising powers.

The Hindu treats the beauty of place in a peculiar way foreign to other peoples: his method of appreciating and celebrating it is quite different and singular. The whole of our Samskrit literature is full of proofs to show with what feelings of reverence the Hindu has been trained to regard the natural beauty of a particular place. To him it is not to suggest any ideas of self-indulgence or social enjoyment of the mere sensuous kind, for it is to him the place for self-restraint, for solitary meditation leading from nature up to nature's God, for the confirmation of pious resolves, the strengthening of the religious fibres. As the late Sister Nivedita well pointed out, had Niagara been situated on the Ganges, how different would have been its valuation by humanity! Instead of picnics and pleasure trips, the perennial pilgrimage of worshipping crowds. Instead of pleasure groves, ashramas, small sylvan homes of hermits. Instead of hotels, temples. Instead of excesses of sensuous indulgence, the simplicity and severity of self-restrained asceticism. Or, instead of treating it as a mighty means to the end of producing economic utilities by the creation of a motive power, a reaction against objectivity, a more absorbing subjectivity, a detachment from the body and the outward material world to feed the life of the spirit.

It is difficult, indeed, to make an exhaustive enumeration of the myriads of sacred spots which an overflowing love of the country has planted throughout India. One of the best lists of these is to be found in the Vanaparva of the *Mahabharata* where two descriptions are given of the principal holy places, one by Narada and the other by Dhaumya. The sixty-sixth chapter of the *Garudapurana* also gives an interesting list, but a most exhaustive one is given in its eighty-first chapter, which passes in review the whole continent from the Himalayas to Cape Comorin in locating the holy places. There are other lists given in the various accounts which we have about what are known as Pithasthanas. The *Tantrachudamani* mentions 52 as their number, while the *Devibhagavata* mentions 108. The *Kubjikatantra* enumerates the various Siddhapithas throughout India. The *Sivacharita* distinguishes 51 Mahapithas from 26 Upapithas. A reference to these holy places is also contained in the *Kalikapurana*.

It is remarkable also to notice that not a single one of these numerous holy places marking the various parts of India, and conferring upon them all a common sanctity, has been situated outside the borders of the mother country. The Hindu has not got to traverse beyond the sacred precincts of his native land to some far-off Palestine to pay homage to any of the numerous (thirty-three crores) deities that constitute his pantheon or to the memory of any of the numerous religious heroes, saints, and seers that have made his country famous. He is too much in love with his own country to think of establishing any tie of allegiance with any foreign country; that would be a violence, as it were, to his spirit of loyalty to his motherland. The patriotism of the Hindu is a very jealous mistress that does not permit him any other external attachments. India is unique in the multiplicity of her cults and creeds, sects and faiths, castes and communities, cultures and religions, but she has also been the cradle-land of each and all of them, the invariable birthplace of their founders and progenitors. The mother-country of the Hindu is extraordinarily self-contained, both physically and spiritually; the aids to noble life are all within her borders; her sons have not to seek elsewhere for religious inspiration or aids to spiritual culture. The mother-country is endowed with an inexhaustible fertility on that score. It is thus that this love of the country has ultimately confined the location of the innumerable shrines and sacred places of India within her geographical limits, and has thus given rise to one of the most remarkable and distinguishing characteristics of ancient Hindu culture and civilisation, demonstrating the Hindu mode of expression of the universal human sentiment of patriotism.

PILGRIMAGE AS FOSTERING PATRIOTISM AND NATIONALISM IN ANCIENT INDIA

THE institution of pilgrimage, besides being the Hindu mode of expression of the universal sentiment of patriotism, is calculated to produce another most remarkable effect upon the national character. It not merely strengthens and sustains the love of the country, which is idealised and glorified into an object of worship for the people, but it also expands their geographical consciousness, which would otherwise be limited to the necessarily narrow horizon of the particular province or locality from which they come. The institution of pilgrimage is undeniably a most powerful factor for developing the geographical sense in the people, which enables them to think and feel that India is not a mere congeries of geographical fragments, but a single, though immense, organism, filled with the tide of one strong pulsating life from end to end. The contemplation of the numerous holy places scattered throughout the vast continent has the inevitable effect of extending the geographical horizon of the unlettered millions for whom much of their religion is objectively rèpresented in the external ceremony of pilgrimage, and they are thus naturally and automatically led to expand the limits of their original narrow home or the land of their birth, and learn to identify it with a gradually widening area over which they are forced to traverse by religious necessities in search of the holy places scattered thoughout it. The institution is thus a most effective agency of popular education in geographical consciousness. The unlettered masses cannot be expected to grasp and care for the abstract truths and philosophy of religion, which do not recognise but always transcend the limitations of space or the religious influences of a particular place. For them religion has to be brought from the skies to the market-place ; it has to be simplified and objectified so that its influences may be brought within the range of popular perception. Pilgrimage has, therefore, been an essentially popular institution meant for the religious education of the masses ; it has grown up in response to the needs of the nation at large and not of its cultured or advanced classes, which may do without it. It is therefore undeniable that, appealing as it does to the vast majority of the people of India, the institution serves as a most powerful agency of popular education, of awakening the popular mind of India to a consciousness of the geographical limits of their country, their real home, the home of homes; of kindling in them a sense of its continental vastness and variety, the immensity of its physical proportions and territorial expansion, of its natural resources, potentialities and possibilities.

Besides, the visit to holy places as an imperative religious duty has made wide travelling a national habit in India in all ages of life, with young and old alike; and considering the special circumstances of travelling in ages anterior to the era of steam and mechanical transport, it could not but have the redeeming characteristic of promoting a deeper and sounder knowledge of the tracts traversed than that which can be acquired by modern globe-trotters availing themselves of the speed and of the conveniences of present-day travelling. We must also recognise that it was this supremely Indian institution in fact which served in the days of yore in place of the modern railway and other facilities for travel to promote popular movements from place to place and active intercourse between parts, producing an intimate knowledge of the whole. We must dismiss once for all the theory that travelling was not popular in ancient India for the mere want of the physical facilities for it. On the contrary, we must attribute to it, as a widespread national habit, the successful propagation of the Indo-Aryan system of civilisation from one end of the country to the other, and the spread of the influence of the innumerable creeds and cultures beyond the original geographical limits of the places of their birth over parts separated from them by great distances. It was thus that the faiths founded by a Gautama Buddha or a Mahavira radiated in all directions from the particular place of their origin. It was thus that the sermon preached at the Deer Park of Sarnath in Benares gradually extended its sway and made itself heard over all parts of India and beyond. It was thus that Sankaracharya was able to accomplish his spiritual *digvijaya* of the entire country from end to end, establishing the pillars of his religious victory, the capitals of his spiritual empire, in the four quarters of India. It was thus that the religions founded by a Ramanuja or a Madhva in the south, or a Chaitanya, a Ramananda, a Kavira or a Nanak in the north, spread themselves beyond the limits of their original and primary influence over much larger areas and peoples. It is thus that we have to attribute the success of the numerous religious or popular movements that characterised the whole course of our history to the fully formed predilection in the masses in favour of wide travelling, which thus triumphed over the physical difficulties of pre-mechanical ages in the way of their having an intimate knowledge of the different parts of the country separated by large distances. It was in a real sense the conquest of matter by mind, the subjection of the physical by the spiritual. India, as a whole, was realised as the mighty motherland by the popular mind in every part of India in spite of an unfavouring natural environment. The system allowed no parochial provincial sense to grow up, which might interfere with the growth of a popular consciousness of the geographical unity of the country; it allowed no sense of physical comforts to stand in the way of the sacred duty of intimately knowing one's native land, and softened the severities of old-world travelling by breaking the pilgrim's route at convenient holy halting-places at short distances.

"Along with this system and network of Hindu holy places should also be considered the multitude of monuments with which Buddhism and Jainism, ultimately and essentially but phases of Hindu thought, have adorned the land and influenced the geographical consciousness of large numbers of people under their direct sway. What the idea of pilgrimage is to the Hindu mind, the worship of relics is to the Buddhist and Jain. The former realised itself in the planting of holy places, the latter in the erection of monuments beautifying the land." We thus find that the loving heart of both the Buddhist and the Jain has marked its appreciation of the sacredness of the whole country by the erection, in all its distant and different parts, of noble and mighty monuments upon which have been cheerfully lavished all the resources of art and the most extravagant expenditure of wealth. "The pillars (lats) at Delhi, Tirhut, Sankisa, Sanchi, etc.; the chaitya-caves and viharas at Bihar, Nasik, Ajanta, Elura, Karle, Kanheri, Bhaja, Bedsa, Dhamnar, Udaigiri, Bagh, etc.; stupas of Manikyala, Sarnath, Sanchi, and Amaravati; the gateways and stone railings at Barahat (Bharhut), Mathura, Gaya, Sanchi and Amaravati; and lastly, the numerous Gandhara monasteries—all these, considering their widely separated locations, point to the extensive area which was unified by a common artistic impulse, a single religious idea."

We thus see that the institution of pilgrimage, besides being one of the characteristic Hindu modes of worship of the country, besides being the Hindu expression of a universal human sentiment, is of very great cultural value in other respects. It is one of the most efficient agencies of popular education and political progress by means of which the mind of the masses, the unlettered millions of India, is automatically emancipated from the limitations of a narrow, provincial, parochial outlook to which it is naturally subjected. It extends the geographical consciousness of the people, the basis of all political progress, by which they are enabled to realise what is their true home, the home of homes, the existence of a common country which they have to love and serve, the physical form of the fatherland claiming their homage.

NATIONALISM IN SAMSKRIT LITERATURE

It is not adequately recognised that the indigenous culture and literature of the country were playing their full part in the development of a sense of Nationalism in the ancient days of Hindu India. There was the system of pilgrimage universally current in India, which was materially aiding in the development of an expanded geographical consciousness in the people that it might be able to grasp the whole country from Kashmir to Cape Comorin as a single unit, as the one indivisible motherland claiming the homage of all her children whatever might be the particular locality of their origin, and as the common theatre of national activity. To every province of India has been allotted its own number of special shrines and sacred places, so that each has had its own part to play primarily in the religious, and subsidiarily —and as a consequence—the political progress of the people. All the provinces of India have been treated under this scheme of pilgrimage, this supremely Indian institution, as members of a common organism consciously co-operating towards the attainment of a common aim, viz. the expansion of the geographical outlook of the unlettered masses, who would otherwise have had their horizon "cabin'd, cribb'd, confined" within the circumscribed limits of their original narrow homes. All parts of India were thus made to serve a common cause and achieve a common ideal, so that a sense of provincial isolation, which finds such a congenial home in the Indian atmosphere and environment, might be struck at the very root, and the way paved for the growth of that larger consciousness of a wider country which is the primary formative factor of Indian nationhood.

But apart from this institution which is the characteristic product of Hindu thought and culture, there were also the vehicles of that thought and that culture to exercise the very same influence and make similar contributions towards the accomplishment of the sacred mission of nation-building in India. It will scarcely win a ready belief and acceptance, and yet it will be no exaggeration, if it is deliberately stated and maintained that India was preaching the gospel of Nationalism when Europe was passing through what has been aptly called the Dark Age of her history, and was labouring under the travails of a new birth. It was truly the Dark Age of Europe, because it was a period of unrest and unsettlement, when she was a prey to the invasions of the barbarians who, leaving their old homes, overran and disorganised the Roman Empire, but were not progressive enough to plant fixed local habitations of their own in place of the old ones they abandoned. Under such circumstances, there could not be any settled life or progress. History hardly shows any important evidence of nomadic peoples developing to any great extent in civilisation until and unless they bound themselves to a fixed habitation and rid themselves of their migratory instincts and habits. The Hebrew people, for instance, in spite of the political training they received from Moses, could not achieve much progress until Joshua settled them in Palestine. "The Athenians under Themistocles saved the State of Athens on their ships, because after the victory they again took possession of their city, but the Teutones and the Cimbri perished because they left their old homes and failed to conquer a new one." True it is that the Jewish people have developed a considerable sense of community without developing a common home and motherland, but we must be ready to admit that the absence of that fundamental physical basis is the main reason why the Jews have failed to form themselves into a political unit or a nation and a recognised factor in world-politics.

There are indeed various factors that co-operate and contribute towards the making of a nation, such as a common language, a common religion, a common government, and a common culture and social economy, but perhaps none of these is such a fundamental and indispensable factor as the evolution of a common country, a fixed definite abode, with sharply defined geographical boundaries. "The spirit, according to Hindu philosophy, clothes itself in the body in and through which it works; it needs a vehicle, an instrument, a physical framework whereby it expresses and outshapes itself in the external world of matter. And it seems as if the same principle also applies in respect of the spirit of Nationality. It seems as if even Nationality needs a material physical basis without which it can hardly manifest and assert itself as a real existence and factor in the political world. The primary requisite for the birth and growth of a nation is the certainty, fixity, and permanence of place, and when *that* is assured, the other formative forces will appear and make themselves felt in due course. A common fatherland is preliminary to all national development: round that living nucleus will naturally gather all those feelings, associations, traditions and other elements which go to make up a people's language and literature, culture and religion, and thereby establish its separate existence and individuality, demanding its preservation and independent development as a valuable cultural unit indispensable to humanity. The unifying influence of a common country, of common natural surroundings, of common economic conditions, is indeed irresistible, and the assertion may be safely made that it will be effectively operative against other disintegrating and dividing forces and factors such as differences in manners and customs, language and religion."

Thus, while Europe was being overrun by the nomads and was struggling to found new homes for her peoples in place of the old ones disorganised and destroyed by the barbarian invasions, when the very conditions of national development had not dawned upon Europe, the gospel of a wholesome Nationalism was already a vital force in the public life of India. All the conditions that make for the growth of a sense of nationhood were fully developed and long known in ancient India. Not only were the original Indo-Aryan invaders in safe and complete possession of a fixed, definite, permanent local habitation for themselves, sharply demarcated from the rest of the world within well-defined and conspicuous geographical boundaries, but the conception and consciousness of this new home had long dawned upon the popular mind. The limits of this vast, newly conquered continent, which was already unified under the discipline of a common culture and civilisation, the perception of the individuality of this immense mother-country, were not merely known to the cultured classes of the Indian community—a knowledge of these had also filtered through the ages down to the lowest strata of society. The Indians as a people had long realised the physical individuality of their mother-country. They were already in possession of the necessary material, tangible, objective basis upon which a sense of Nationalism might be built up.

Towards the performance of this truly stupendous task, namely, that of moulding and developing the national consciousness of a country of continental proportions, the indigenous vehicles of culture played a worthy and glorious part. It is a mistake readily to assume that the origin of that remarkable social phenomenon of Nationalism is to be found in the West; that it is a genuinely Western product imported into the Eastern countries long after their growth and development; that the Eastern mind was completely a stranger to the very conception of the mother-country, a sense of natural attachment to her, and a corresponding sense of duties and obligations which the children of the soil owe to her. Such misconceptions are due to a colossal ignorance of the culture of the East. Even in the dim and distant age of remote antiquity, unillumined by the light of historical knowledge, we find the underlying principles of Nationalism chanted forth in the hymns of the *Rigveda* embodying the very first utterance of humanity itself. That book, one of the oldest literary records of humanity, reveals conscious and fervent attempts made by the Rishis, those profoundly wise organisers of Hindu polity and culture, to visualise the unity of their mother-country, nay, to transfigure the mother earth into a living deity and enshrine her in the loving heart of the worshipper. This is best illustrated by the famous river hymn, in which are invoked in an impassioned prayer the various rivers of the Punjab, which were eminently entitled to the nation's gratitude for their invaluble contributions towards the material making of their motherland. As the mind of the devotee calls up in succession the images of these different rivers defining the limits of his country, it naturally traverses the entire area of his native land and grasps the image of the whole as a visible unit and form. Certainly a better and simpler, a more effective and soul-stirring formula could not be invented for the perception of the fatherland as the indivisible unit than the following prayer:

> "O ye Ganga, Yamuna, Sarasvati, Satadru, and Parusni, receive ye my prayers! O ye Marutbridha joined by the Asikni, Vitasta, and Arjikiya joined by the Sushoma, hear ye my prayers!"

It calls up at once in the mind's eye a picture of the whole of Vedic India, and fulfils in a remarkable way the poet's purpose behind it of awakening the people to a sense of the fundamental unity of their country. The river hymn of the *Rigveda*, therefore, presents the first national conception of Indian unity such as it was. It was necessarily conditioned by the geographical horizon reached in that age, as indicated by these and other geographical data.

The pattern and the fashion thus set in the *Rigveda*, whereby a knowledge of the country was sought to be spread through its association in daily prayers, were naturally followed by the later literature, which is always indissolubly bound up with the Vedic tradition and truths. Thus the following Pauranic prayer is but an adaptation of the Vedic hymn to a new environment, to an expanded geographical horizon embracing the whole of India within its limits :

> "O ye Ganga, Yamuna, Godaveri, Sarasvati, Narmada, Sindhu, and Cauvery, come ye and enter into this water of my offering."

This holy text for the sacrificial purification of water is daily repeated as a mantram by millions of devout Hindus all over the country during their baths and worship, and cannot fail to lift them above the limitations of their ordinary domestic homes to a higher and a wider plane of thought on which they can realise the bond of brotherhood which connects them all as citizens of a vaster country, the fundamental unity of the whole of India welding together its distant and different parts into a common indivisible whole. The mental horizon embracing the limited interests of the domestic circle or an individual home or a petty village, naturally expands under the influence and inspiration of such prayers, so that it comes to embrace the wider interests of a far more extended and glorified home, of the vast nation-family in which are merged the individual families.

The same ennobling, elevating effect is produced on the national consciousness by the following Pauranic couplet, in which the whole of India is presented before the mind's eye as the land of seven mountains which distinguish the several different parts of India and unify them in the physical configuration of a common country: "Mahendra, Malaya, Sahya, Suktiman, Riksa, Vindhya, Pariyatra—these are the seven main hills of India."

Equally efficacious is the following text in enfranchising the mind from the limitations of a narrow, provincial, parochial outlook and awakening it to a vision of the whole country, of which all parts are equally sacred and entitled to homage: "Ayodhya, Mathura, Maya, Kasi, Kanchi, Avanti, and Dvaravati—these are the seven places conferring liberation on the pilgrim."

Here India is represented as the land of seven principal sacred places which it is incumbent on every devotee to visit, and which cover between them practically the entire area of the country. The man who wants salvation is enjoined to regard these sacred cities in seven different and distant parts of India with an equal eye of impartiality and to attach to all of them the same degree of sanctity. Just as the bathers in the sacred streams of the Indus and Ganges are united to the bathers in the distant waters of the Narmada and the Cauvery in the utterance of a common prayer producing the sameness of spirit and sentiment born of contemplation of a common country, a consequent sense of brotherhood, of a common nation family, similarly the citizens of Kasi and Kanchi, Avanti and Ayodhya, are made to join hands in a common worship and, though physically apart, are united in spirit. Space divides, but the soul unites !

THE NATIONALISM OF HINDU SECTS

Each of the principal sects of Hinduism has developed its own appropriate prayers and slokas meant for the masses, but they all breathe a common sense of Nationalism and are inspired by the same ideal and aim, viz. the expansion of the limited physical outlook of the worshippers concerned so that they may be led by different roads to the same goal and destination, the constant consciousness of a common home, of the whole of India as the common motherland of all, despite differences of caste and creed. All the subordinate sects of Hinduism stand on the common platform of a larger outlook, an imperial conception of the geographical integrity and individuality of the mighty motherland; all the creeds have a common catholicity so far as a devotion to the motherland, a sense of its complete sacredness, are concerned—the sacredness not merely of the whole, but of each and all of its parts. All the subordinate faiths of Hinduism unite in recognising the essential and primary truth that no real religious progress can be achieved until and unless those limitations and barriers are broken down which are created by the mere physical factor of space, and which divide and isolate men from one another by virtue of the mere distance of their local habitations. For religious progress ultimately means the progress of the expansion of the limited self, and a progressive realisation of its affinity towards others in spite of superficial and temporary differences. And so our Sastras have recognised this cramping influence of the mere physical environment, and have sought to invent appropriate antidotes to it by introducing to the people the conception of a greatly extended geographical horizon, whereby their mental outlook might be broadened and a step gained towards the achievement of final liberation or emancipation.

Thus if one is a Saiva, the Sastras present before him the necessity of his cultivation of the conception of the totality of that vast area throughout which are scattered the various places consecrated to the worship of the great God Siva. If he wants to be a genuine devotee of his God, he must visit all these various places, each of which has been exalted into a holy place for its association with one out of the innumerable aspects of the deity. It looks as if the Viratamurti of the Lord is to be realised through the preliminary process of realising it on a smaller scale in the total extent of the sacred space which, on earth, is associated with Him. Hence the Sastras enjoin upon every devout Saiva the necessity of daily contemplating the numerous places of Saiva worship. They are thus enumerated in a passage selected at random :

> "Somanatha, Srisaila, Mallikarjuna, Ujjaini, Amareswara, Kedara, Dakini, Varanasi, Gaumati, Chitabhumi, Dwaraka, Setubandha, Sivalaya."

Similarly for the Vaishnava are singled out innumerable sacred places distributed throughout the country in all its four quarters, so that he may be trained in a wider geographical consciousness and made to identify himself with the interests of a much larger country transcending the narrow limitations of his original place of birth. A process of expansion of the mere physical outlook is preliminary to all mental and spiritual expansion. And so a phase or aspect of the great deity has been stamped upon each of the various sacred places consecrated to Him, and the devotee who does not realise by a personal visit the special sacredness of each is likely to miss something of the stupendous significance which can only dawn upon the consciousness of the pilgrim who acquires the personal experience of all of them. Passages in our Sastras bearing on the lists of places sacred to Vishnu mention too many names to be conveniently enumerated here. Between them they cover the whole area of the country from Badari in the north through Ayodhya and Mathura, Kasi and Dwaraka, to Jagannath and Sriranga.

The worshipper of Sakti is also similarly enjoined to cultivate the conception of the extensive physical space consecrated to the worship of Kali, the Mother. "In the story of Sati, the perfect wife, who can miss the significance of the fifty-two places in which fragments of Her smitten body fell? One finger fell in Calcutta which is still the Kalighat; and the tongue fell at Kangra or Jwalamukhi in the north Punjab, and appears to this day as a licking tongue of fire from underneath the ground; and the left finger fell at Benares, where it is still Annapurna, the giver of bread."

Thus, whether the Hindu is a Saiva, or a Vaishnava, or a Sakta in his choice of the special mode of his spiritual culture, he is bound to cultivate in common with all his co-religionists the sense of an expanded geographical consciousness, which alone can contribute to the expansion of his mind and soul. Indeed, it has been rightly assumed and asserted that the physical geography of India has partially influenced her history and shaped and moulded the course of her culture and civilisation. As the old Aryan invaders of India first set foot upon her soil, there burst into view upon their eyes the vast territorial expansion of the country, imposing no limits upon the progress of their colonisation. India in the eyes of these early settlers and missionaries was a world unto herself, knowing of no bounds in any direction. An infinite stretch of territory produced naturally a psychology, a philosophy, that was easily dominated by a sense of the infinite and the eternal. Thus the geographical sense has aided in the development of the special spiritual sense that is the characteristic of Hindu thought and culture, of Hindu mind with its special gift of a synthetic vision. Thus the physical conditions of spiritual development were fully recognised and taken advantage of by the founders of the various sects and creeds of India, who always sought to present before their respective followers through appropriate formulæ the widest possible geographical horizon, with its inevitable effects upon their mental outlook.

Along with the special prayers for the various faiths aiming at the presentation of the conception of the entire country as a single geographical unit, one indivisible whole, of which all the parts were equally sacred and essential, organic and integral, there were again certain regulations prescribed for the performance of the ceremonies common to all Hindus irrespective of their particular faiths, which also would appear on a close examination and analysis to produce the same effect and to aim at the very same ideal. I mean the regulations prescribed in our Smritis regarding the performance of the most universal of the Hindu ceremonies, which is indeed one of the fundamental distinguishing marks separating Hindu society from all other societies of the world. Those regulations prescribe certain places where alone it is recommended that the sraddha should be performed, and in the geographical distribution of these places we shall find that there is not a single part of the vast Indian continent which has been ignored and excluded. A good list of the places is to be found in the *Vishnu Smriti*, where they are mentioned in the following order :—

1. Pushkara in Northern Rajputana. A sraddha done at Pushkara will, it is stated, bear eternal fruits ; and by bathing there, one is immediately absolved of all sins.
2. Gaya.

3. The place of the Akshayavata, one of which is traced in Behar, and another at Allahabad.
4. The hill of Amarakantaka, which is on the Mekhala mountain in the Vindhya range.
5. Varaha hill in the Sambalpur division.
6. Anywhere on the banks of the Narmada.
7. Anywhere on the banks of the Yamuna.
8. Specially anywhere on the banks of the Ganga.
9. Kusavarta on the mountain called Tryambaka, where the Godaveri takes its rise.
10. Binduka in the Deccan.
11. Nilaparvata.
12. Kanakhala near Hardwar.
13. Kubjamra, which is the name of a plain in Orissa.
14. Bhrigutunga, which is the name of a mountain near the Amarakantaka in the Himalayas.
15. Kedara, the famous peak of the Himalayas.
16. Mahalaya mountain.
17. Nadantika river.
18. Sugandha river.
19. Sakambhari, identified with modern Shambar in Rajputana.
20. The sacred place on the Phalgu.
21. Mahaganga, which is another name of the Alakananda.
22. Trihalikagrama near Salagrama.

23. Kumaradhara, which is the name of a lake in Kashmir. According to the *Vayupurana*, the lake was created by the God Kumara by a stroke of his arrow causing water to stream forth from the Krauncha mountain.
24. Prabhasa.
25. Anywhere on the banks of the river Sarasvati.
26. Hardwar.
27. Prayaga.
28. The mouths of the Ganga.
29. Naimisaranya.
30. Benares.

This list gives the names of the various places marked out for the proper performance of the sraddha, and it will be seen that in their selection every part of India has been drawn upon and represented. There are again special rivers mentioned, such as the Godaveri, Gaumati, the Vetravati of Central India ; the Vipasa, the Vitasta, the Satadru, and the Chandrabhaga, the Irawadi and the Sindhu of the Punjab ; the five rivers of the South, viz. the Krishna, the Vena, the Tunga, the Bhadra, and the Kona. Without multiplying further passages, the one just quoted from the *Vishnu Smriti* will suffice to bear out the truth of the contention herein urged, viz. that the underlying principle of the determination of these sacred places was to treat the entire country as a single sacred unit and spread the conception of such sacredness among the unlettered millions of India, who were all to think of these holy places in connection with the performance of that ceremony which has had the widest possible, nay, universal currency among the Hindus as a people, whatever might be the special sects or creeds to which they belonged. Besides, we should also recognise the other great influence exercised upon the minds of those who perform the ceremony of sraddha at any of these sacred places. The performance of the funeral ceremony naturally creates a vital bond of association and connection which will bind for ever the unfortunate performer of that ceremony with the new place far away from his own native land, and by virtue of this association with his dear departed ones the new and unfamiliar spot comes to have a most familiar and cherished place in the heart of the man himself. In this way are broken down the physical barriers of space which would otherwise restrict considerably his geographical horizon or the extent of the country in which he takes a personal interest. A much wider area now dawns upon his geographical consciousness, in which he comes to feel an intense personal interest due to new associations connected with the performance of melancholy duties.

Thus, like the institution of pilgrimage itself, the geographical basis fixed by our Sastras for the other institution of the sraddhas will have the effect of producing ultimately the same effects as we have noticed in connection with the working of the former system, viz. training the mind of the people, unlettered and uncultured, in the easiest and the most natural manner, in habits of conception of the physical limits of the vast motherland which would be otherwise incapable of comprehension by the untutored minds.

We have thus seen how our ancient culture, and Samskrit literature, in which that culture is represented, have throughout contributed towards the creation of that primary factor of nationalism, viz. the sense of the possession of a common country to love and to serve, to live for and to die for, of which the different parts are to be regarded with a feeling of uniform sacredness as essential members co-operating towards the good of the common whole. We have here, as it were, a scheme of religious decentralisation, akin to administrative decentralisation, by means of which numerous religious centres have been created throughout the length and breadth of the country for the development of a high level of spiritual culture, even as in the adminstrative sphere we find the creation of innumerable centres of local autonomy by means of which a high level of public spirit, political consciousness and progress is sought to be created, and, in the sphere of the military, forts and garrisons set up at various centres to distribute the military power of the realm evenly among its different parts so as to make its influence uniformly felt throughout the country.

NATIONALISM AS A HINDU POLITICAL IDEAL

Just as Hindu religion has been instrumental in spreading the conception of a common fatherland in the whole of India from the Himalayas to Cape Comorin among the masses by means of appropriate prayers, ceremonies, and obligatory visits to the numerous places of pilgrimage which do not recognise at all the divisions of provinces, similarly Hindu politics in ancient times also did not encourage the growth of any narrow notions limiting the extent of the motherland. The success of the early missionaries of Aryan culture in propagating it throughout the continent signalised itself by its designation by the single name of Bharatavarsha, after the name of the eponymous hero Bharata who was the embodiment of the culture of his race. The name Bharatavarsha is thus not a mere geographical expression like the term India, having only a physical reference, but it has a deep historical significance. It signifies the complete accomplishment of the work initiated by the Aryan forefathers of colonising the whole country and bringing its different parts under the unifying discipline of a common culture and civilisation. Bharatavarsha is thus another name for Aryanised and Hinduised India, betokening the conquest of a new thought and a new faith with their special means of self-expression developed through appropriate literature, disciplines, and institutions, social, economical, and political. Thus, the application of a single individualising appellation to a vast stretch of territory with parts divided by endless varieties and peopled by many races, speaking many tongues, professing many faiths and owning many cultures, was the first step taken towards the assimilation of the entire country as the one indivisible motherland and the living objective of national service. But this process of assimilating was also aided by politics. A sense of possession is always followed by a sense of appropriation, utilisation, and enjoyment. Accordingly it became the natural and legitimate ideal of the Hindu king in ancient India to make the area of his authority coincide with that of the whole country, to make his actual jurisdiction embrace the entire territory which he morally claimed as his own native land. Thus the establishment of an undisputed and paramount sovereignty of the whole of India up to the limits of the ocean became the objective of kingly activity in ancient times. The ideal is thus put forward by the sacred work *Aitareya Brahmana* :

> " Monarchy at its highest should have an empire extending right up to natural boundaries ; it should be territorially all-embracing up to the very ends uninterrupted, and should constitute and establish one state and administration in the land up to the seas."

The territorial synthesis leads the way to the political synthesis, and is in turn emphasised by it. The evolution of the name Bharatavarsha was inevitably followed by its natural political consequences in the assimilation of the physical area implied by it to the indigenous political authority or system.

It is thus a mistake to suppose that the conception of paramount sovereignty is something strange to Hindu political thought and was imported into India from foreign countries. It has even been asserted that the founder of the Mauryan Empire was only imitating the models and methods set by the Achæmenian Empire of Persia. It is however forgotten that, long before the days of that Persian Empire, the ideal of political suzerainty was preached in all the sacred works of Hindus as a perfectly legitimate and laudable ideal to be realised by the Kshatriya kings of ancient India. If terms or names are to be taken as symbols of realities, if a mere word cannot grow except on the basis of some fact accomplished, then the abundance of the various terms, names, and words indicative of overlordship or suzerainty in Vedic literature is highly significant. A reference to the several Vedic concordances and indexes will show the various passages in which are to be found the uses of such definitely significant terms as "Adhiraja," "Rajadhiraja," "Samraj," "Ekaraj," and even "Sarvabhauma"; but lest we doubt the reality and the substance behind these terms and symbols, we are confronted by the remarkable fact that there were special ceremonies developed in connection with the inauguration and installation of such paramount sovereignty, of which elaborate details and descriptions are preserved in some of our most sacred works which concern themselves solely with religious realities, with rites and institutions, and not with imaginative inventions having no application in actual life. Probably the most confirmed and extreme prejudice against Hindu culture and Samskrit literature cannot lay the charge against our sacred works like the *Aitareya Brahmana* or *Satapatha Brahmana* that their contents have no connection with life and its actual practices, but partake of the character of poetry or fiction, as a type of literary composition. The truth of the matter is that the serious and sincere way in which those particular ceremonies are treated of in our sacred works cannot but justify our claiming for them a complete reality which was perfectly attainable and frequently attained in those days. The sacred books generally speak of three characteristic ceremonies, viz. those of the Vajapeya, the Rajasuya, and the Asvamedha, of which the performance can only be claimed by a king who succeeds by means of his conquest in making himself the king of kings. For minute details and descriptions of these ceremonies the reader is referred to *Satapatha Brahmana*, *Aitareya Brahmana*, *Katyayana Srauta Sutra*, *Asvalayana Srauta Sutra*, *Taittiriya Sanhita*, *Taittiriya Brahmana*, *Sankhyayana Srauta Sutra*, *Atharvaveda*, *Maitrayani Sanhita*, *Kathaka Sanhita*, *Vajasaneyi Sanhita*, all of which are invested in the Hindu mind with a degree of sanctity and seriousness in the face of which it will be a sacrilege and a profanation for us to regard them as books merely meant for the cultivation of the imagination and not serving the actual purposes of life. The Hindu religious books are all practical books comprising details of ceremonies actually performed by the Hindus in prosecution of the ideals laid down therein. We cannot, therefore, light-heartedly reject the evidence of our religious literature regarding the ceremonies connected with Imperial coronations and their necessary political significance.

Along with these terms and ceremonies indicative of the conception of an all-India overlordship the books fortunately preserve for us lists of kings who are said to have succeeded in carrying the conception into actual execution. Lists of such paramount kings are to be found in the *Aitareya Brahmana*, the *Satapatha Brahmana*, the *Sankhyayana Srauta Sutra*, the *Mahabharata*, and most of the Puranas. It is not possible to establish the historicity of all these great kings of old according to the accepted standards of accuracy and scientific criticism. But the lists are highly significant as embodying a genuine tradition about the realisation in ancient India of the legitimate Kshatriya ideal of an undisputed sovereignty over the whole of India up to the seas. Besides, one of the three ceremonies, viz. Asvamedha, can claim its actual performances in perfectly historical times. The historical list of Asvamedhins in Indian history includes the following names:

1. Pushyamitra.
2. Samudragupta.
3. Kumaragupta.
4. Adityasena.
5. Pulakesi II.

The theory has, therefore, to be definitely abandoned that the conception of paramount sovereignty was unknown to ancient India until it was realised by Chandragupta Maurya. We can at least claim that the idea itself was much older than the Mauryan Emperor, who need not have gone to far-off Persia for inspiration and guidance in the matter of accomplishing his projected political unification of as much of the country as possible. The sacred works preserved for him a rich storehouse of national tradition on the subject, the glorious record of many an illustrious hero who preceded him in the work of bringing the whole of India under the 'umbrella' of one central authority. In the historical period we have, besides Chandragupta Maurya, no less than three successive kings, each of whom attained the political status of becoming the king of kings, viz :

1. Asoka.
2. Samudragupta.
3. Harshavardhana.

The cyclical reappearance of these overlordships in the course of Indian history served to keep clear and fresh in the popular consciousness a sense of the unity and individuality of the mother-country as it uttered itself in politics, just as it has always been kept clear and fresh by means of religion. Thus both politics and religion helped to fix in the popular mind of ancient India the consciousness of the possession of a common country to live and to serve, which is the primary and indispensable basis of an abiding nationalism.

SAMSKRIT LITERATURE AND ITS BEARING ON NATIONAL LIFE

If we agree as to the harmonious development of national life in all its phases and aspects in ancient India in the twofold domain of material and spiritual progress, there will be no difficulty in our accepting the position that Samskrit literature, which was the indigenous vehicle of the culture of the country in ancient times, was also possessed of those elements and resources which enabled it to minister adequately to the manifold interests of a wholesome national development. So far as the interests of religious and spiritual life are concerned, it is universally admitted that Samskrit literature was more than able to fulfil its proper part in that regard. It is, however, forgotten that Samskrit literature is not exclusively religious or philosophical in its character. It may be assumed on mere *a priori* grounds that it could not but have fulfilled in a large measure the material ends of national life in the ancient days of Hindu India, when the country was culturally self-contained and independent to a very large extent, so that the mental aids to her material development must have been supplied by her own indigenous literatures.

So far as the ends of a healthy national development are concerned, the most fundamental consideration is a living consciousness of a common country, born of an intimate knowledge of its different parts, culminating in an acute sense of nationalism, finding in the whole country the material basis of its activity. It has been already demonstrated that Samskrit literature is specially efficacious in creating a sense of attachment to the mother-country akin to religious devotion in its fervour, and a consequent larger conception and mental outlook, which are essential to nation-building in a country like India with its special problems and conditions. But besides supplying this indispensable basis of nationalism and ensuring its growth on a most solid foundation—the foundation of abiding religious sentiments and convictions—the cause of national development in various directions was also amply served by the literature of the country in ancient days. We can claim on the basis of undisputed facts and the testimony of trustworthy history and the researches of Western scholars that in point of economic progress and material development ancient India won for herself an honoured place in the comity of nations of the old world, and we may therefore assume the necessary progress and development of an adequate literature together with an appropriate educational machinery and organisation by which such progress and development were achieved. But apart from this *a priori* assumption, we may also point to certain facts about the existence of such works in Samskrit as have a direct bearing on material welfare.

The indigenous principle of classification of the manifold ends of national life divided them into four principal departments, designated as Dharma, Artha, Kama, and Moksha. Round each of these departments naturally developed its appropriate literature. Of these we need not refer in this connection to the literature bearing upon Moksha or spiritual emancipation, for the strength of Samskrit literature in this regard is admitted on all hands, and is too well known to need any elaboration on the present occasion ; but we may try to indicate in a broad survey the quantity and the quality of the literature that is available in relation to the other topics.

Firstly, as regards Artha, or material welfare proper, we may point out that Samskrit literature considers it under the following four principal divisions, each of which embraced quite a variety of subjects and works, as shown below :—

(*a*) Agriculture, under which were also included all the subsidiary or allied occupations and sciences that go with it, such as farming, horticulture, sericulture, botany, zoology, with special reference to cattle-rearing, physiography, meteorology, and the like. These various subjects are called by the indigenous names of Krishividya, Vanaspatisastram, Kosakarakeetavidya, Pasupalya, Bhusastram, Rituvidya, and the like. Each of these subjects has developed a voluminous literature of its own, but unfortunately much of that literature is lost, and the portion that is available is still mostly in manuscript awaiting publication. For instance, references are to be found to works on botany known as Vrikshayurveda ; to works on horses, or Asvasastra, of which the traditional authority is Salihotra ; to works on elephants, or Gajasastra, of which the traditional authority is Palakapya ; and so forth. But the works themselves cannot be traced. An account of the speculation of the Hindus on the subject of botany is to be found in the work of a most learned scholar of modern times, viz. *The Positive Sciences of the Ancient Hindus*, by Dr Brajendranath Seal.

(*b*) Secondly, there was the division called Varta, which embraced commerce and its allied occupations, and subjects called by the indigenous names of Vittasastram, Dravyagunam, Vanijyavidya, etc. In such monumental works as the *Arthasastra* of Kautilya and the *Brihat-Sanhita* of Varahamihra we have chapters giving detailed accounts of the economic products of India.

(*c*) There was a division called Silpa, which comprised all the subjects belonging to the twofold division of pure and applied science. It thus included mathematics, physics, astronomy, and other subjects connected with the various arts and crafts of civilised life. It may not be out of place in this connection to record the achievements made by the Hindus in these various scientific and practical subjects. In arithmetic the world owes the decimal notation to the Hindus. Algebra was represented by such well-known names as Aryabhatta and Bhaskaracharya. The solution of quadratic equations was first made by the Hindus, who were also the first to apply algebra to astronomical investigation and geometrical demonstrations. Geometry arose in India in connection with the construction of altars and their enclosures according to the various figures. Trigonometry is also the special invention of the Hindus, and Bhaskara wrote a book on spherical trigonometry. Astronomy was represented by many famous names, such as those of Aryabhatta, the author of *Suryasiddhanta*, who boldly maintained the rotation of the earth on its axis and explained the true cause of the eclipses of the sun and moon. In his *Golapada* he gives us the names of the twelve divisions of the solar zodiac. His calculation of the earth's circumference was fairly accurate. He was followed by Varahamihra, the famous author of *Brihat-Sanhita*, and by Brahmagupta, the author of *Brahmasphutasiddhanta*, in which he ascertained the calculations of lunar and solar eclipses, the position of the moon's cusps, and the conjunctions of the planets and the stars. After Brahmagupta came Bhaskara, the author of *Siadhanta-Siromani*. Dr Seal's book just mentioned explains the Hindu speculations on physics.

As regards the many arts and crafts which were the necessary handmaids of civilisation, the progress made in ancient India is a matter of history. Though it is difficult to substantiate it by reference to extant literary works bearing on them, yet their existence in ancient times cannot be disputed. There are references to the sixty-four fine arts in many works, all of which were taught in the ancient Indian universities like Taxila.

(*d*) Lastly, there was a fourth division called Ayurveda, under which were included the various branches of medical science, including pharmacy, surgery, anatomy, osteology, chemistry, physiology, etc. In the medical sciences the most famous names are those of Charaka and Susruta, the founders of the Ayurvedic system of medicine, which is still holding its own against the other medical systems of the world. An account of Hindu achievements in the domain of anatomy and osteology is given in the works of Dr Seal and Dr Hoernle. Progress in pharmacy is established by the efficacy of the various medicines prescribed by the Ayurvedic system. As regards the progress of Hindu chemistry we have the two original and monumental volumes by the renowned chemist, Dr P. C. Ray of Calcutta.

The second division that we shall consider is what is known in the Sastras as Kama, which is used in a broad sense to mean practically Kala, or the arts. Under this may be included such variety of subjects as grammar, philology, literature, prosody, rhetoric, criticism, logic, history, and so forth, of which the indigenous names are Siksha, Kalpa, Vyakarana, Nirukta, Chhanda, Jyotisha, Itihasa, Purana, Kavya, Sahitya, etc. There is a history of the literature bearing on each subject which is represented by various works. The subject of grammar, for instance, in Samskrit literature is represented by many works and many schools of grammar, each of which has developed various commentaries.

The last division of learning is called by the name of Dharma, which is used in a broad and special sense to mean the code of regulations and laws both for the social and political organisation. Our ancient Sastras recognised the fundamental importance of the family to the nation ; they held that a healthy national life could not be built except on the basis of a healthy domestic life, and accordingly they gave themselves to a systematic and scientific study of sociology. Elaborate regulations and restrictions have been laid down in Smritis, which address themselves to all possible aspects of the social and domestic life, and govern the various relations in which human beings can stand to one another as members of a community. Family life is indeed the basis of national life ; the nation is the glorified family, the expanded family, the family writ large. The recognition of this fundamental principle of nation-building is the real reason why we have such a singularly elaborate literature bearing on domestic and social organisation, the like of which is not to be found in any other literature of the world. The Smritis constitute a unique type of literature, the like of which is not to be found in any other country, and form one of the most characteristic products of Hindu culture. The importance of the discipline of domestic life was so deeply felt and widely appreciated that it probably influenced even the mind of the great Rishi poet Valmiki in his choice of the subject of his monumental masterpiece, the *Ramayana*, for the most important aspect of the *Ramayana* is not the heroic or the historical but the domestic. It is the representation of an idealised domestic life ; we find in it the mirror of domestic perfections, the pattern of domestic manners and virtues by which the domestic life of humanity may be safely governed. The *Ramayana* really represents the ideal father, the ideal mother, the ideal son, the ideal husband, the ideal wife, the ideal brother, the ideal master, the ideal devotee, the ideal friend, in the persons of the various characters that are introduced in the epic. The *Ramayana* is, therefore, one of the greatest moral forces that have been moulding the domestic life of the Hindu community from time immemorial up to the present day ; and, whatever might be their status in the modern political world, it will be admitted on all hands that, in point of felicities of the domestic life and the successful organisation of the family as the unit of society and the State, the Hindus do not lag behind any of the progressive and politically independent nations of the earth, for the culture that goes to the making of a happy family and a well-developed domestic life has been the national possession of the Hindus from a very remote antiquity.

There are various works in Samskrit literature treating of such subjects as Sadachara, Sadharana Dharma, Srautakritya, Samskaravidhi, Prayaschitta, etc., which are all connected with the various aspects and possible phases of the family or domestic life.

Along with the social organisation the regulation of the political organisation was also included within the purview of the various Sastras bearing on Dharma, and the books relating to the regulations of the State are generally known by the technical term of Nitisastras. There are various books, mostly in manuscript, bearing on polity, and my esteemed friend and pupil, Kumara Narendranath Law, M.A., B.L., Premchand Roychand Scholar of Calcutta, has lately prepared an exhaustive list of numerous manuscripts and works traced on this subject. Among the extant publications we may mention the three monumental works, viz. the *Arthasastra* of Kautilya, the *Kamandaki*, and the *Sukranitisara* ; but we know how each of these authorities refers to a multiplicity of authors and schools of thought preceding it. Kautilya, for instance, speaks of ten different schools of political thought that preceded him, and on every minor topic he always quotes the opinions of his predecessors for purposes either of precedent or criticism.

It may be objected that these works on polity possessed only a theoretical importance, and embodied ideal precepts and maxims which were never applied to the actual conditions of political life or to the solution of actual administrative problems. An answer to this criticism will, however, be easily found if we simply consider the character of the most important of the Hindu works on political science and statecraft, namely, the *Arthasastra* of Kautilya. The majority of Western scholars have been agreed as to the authenticity, to the authorship and the age of that remarkable literary production, the discovery and publication of which the world owes to the Government of Mysore. No scholar can reasonably doubt that the author of the work was no other than Chanakya, the first minister of Chandragupta, the Mauryan Emperor, who was materially assisted by him in the foundation and governance of his vast empire, which presented, on account of its extraordinary physical extent and the accompanying variety of conditions, most complex and difficult administrative problems that could only be satisfactorily grappled with and solved by a man of Chanakya's genius and encyclopædic erudition. Unlike Aristotle's *Politics* or Plato's *Republic*, the *Arthasastra* presents a judicious combination of theoretical discussion with practical illustrations of political principles and details of administration, and a predominant note of realism which is born only of a living experience of actual problems and contact with facts. All the familiar problems and topics of administration which claim the attention of the modern Governments of the world find their due treatment in the ancient book. We have chapters devoted to the consideration of such eternal topics of Indian administration as forests, mines, irrigation, famine, land revenue, census, central and local governments, cattle and live stock, agriculture and commerce, arts and crafts, and public finance; and it would appear from the treatment of each of these topics that the author was not merely an academic expert in political theories, but also a most practical administrator, whose generalisations were drawn from a wide area of experience, who was in touch with all the various departments of administration, the heads of which seem to have supplied him with materials and facts which have been incorporated in the book itself by the author as the first minister.

We have now given a rough idea of the secular branches of Samskrit literature which in the ancient days of Hindu India were found capable of ministering to the various practical ends and interests of a wholesome national life and development, by virtue of which India was enabled to a large extent to claim and maintain for a long time a predominant position in the ancient commercial world. We are always in the habit of confining our attention exclusively to the religious and philosophical branches of Samskrit literature, the dazzling splendour of which should not blind us to its other branches, which were also fairly well developed. It is high time that a school of scholars should grow up who will devote themselves assiduously to the sacred task of vindicating the ancient culture of the country, which was not at all found wanting in the matter of promoting the harmonious development of the entire nation in all the manifold fields of human activity, material and moral, secular and spiritual, physical and religious.

THE CULTURAL EQUIPMENT OF SAMSKRIT LITERATURE

To Samskrit literature was given the mission and function of ministering to the harmonious development of ancient India in the different fields of national activity, so far as that development could be accomplished by means of intellectual instruments, literary and cultural aids. What English literature is to the growth of the English people, that was Samskrit literature in relation to the growth of the Hindus. It is difficult in modern times to estimate precisely the magnitude, importance, and value of the part played by Samskrit literature in the material and moral development of the country in the days of its ancient history, for now we find that towards the same end are co-operating quite a number of languages and literatures with English in the central and dominant position, which are all vying with one another in extending their sphere of action and influence. In ancient times, however, Samskrit was the sole medium of communication of the cultured classes, the only vehicle of higher learning and culture in the community, and was thus enjoying for ages an unchallenged monopoly in supplying the nation with all the mental and intellectual aids that were necessary for its development in the two broadly distinguished spheres of material and spiritual progress. Accordingly, we find that Samskrit literature has also grown with the growth of the nation ; it has grown in response to the developing requirements of a wholesome national life that was winning for the country an honoured place in the old-world comity of nations. It has gone on gaining in vastness and variety, width and depth, with the ever-expanding stream of national life. It is this correspondence of the literature to the life of the country that explains the phenomenal variety of Samskrit literature, the variety which is but a reflection of the variety of achievements accomplished by the people whose literature it was. In the first place, as has been already pointed out, we must dismiss the cheap assumption widely made that Samskrit literature is principally religious and philosophical in its character. It is of course true that the religious and philosophical branches of Samskrit literature are the richest in the world, but this extraordinary growth in one direction should not blind us to its growth in other directions also. On this point it is also to be remembered that Samskrit literature contains within itself not only the religious literature of the Hindus proper and Brahmanas, but also of the Buddhists and the Jains. Being thus the chosen vehicle of expression of three such important religions of the world, it is no wonder that the religious side of Samskrit literature appeals to us with a most powerful effect on account of its magnitude and bulk. But, as has been pointed out above, the very mission of Samskrit literature during the ages in which it was the unrivalled vehicle of the country accounts for its remarkable variety and the vastness of its volume. With regard to the variety, I may just give a rough idea by referring to the principal topics on which there are important Samskrit works available. We have intentionally excluded from our purview the works bearing on Moksha or spiritual culture. The most remarkable work bearing on the practical departments of national life is Kautilya's *Arthasastra* cited above, and it is now too well known to need any description of its contents. It is at once a work on economics and politics regarded both as science and art. Next to this work we may mention the almost equally remarkable work, Vatsayana's *Kamasutra*, in which there is a most interesting chapter on regulations concerning domestic economy, including such topics as the kitchen, the kitchen garden, the stores, etc. The next similar work is the *Brihat-Sanhita* of Varahamihra, which is replete with information about the secular aspects of national welfare. There is, again, quite a rich crop of literature bearing upon the exact and abstract sciences, like arithmetic, algebra, trigonometry, geometry, and the concrete sciences, like astronomy, medicine, anatomy, physics, chemistry. Some of the renowned books on metaphysics contain much of physics. Similarly, much literature has undoubtedly grown round each of the sixty-four fine arts to which we have a constant reference in Samskrit works. For instance, as Mahamahopadhyaya Haraprasad Sastry has shown, music itself claims an extensive literature. Bhuvanananda Kavikanthabharana of Bengal, who was a contemporary of Sher Shah, wrote an encyclopædic work giving an account of the eighteen sciences of the Hindus, in which he gives a separate account of music and mentions scores of authors of musical works who flourished in ancient times. Similarly, dancing as an art is treated of by Kohala in several chapters in his work on the *Natyasastra*, which explains the various motions connected with that art. Kohala also mentions the various schools of dramatic art that preceded him, each school having developed its own sutras, bhashyas, vartikas, niruktas, sangrahas, and karikas. In the field of history we may mention *Harshacharita*, *Rajatarangini*, *Ramacharita*, *Navavikramarkacharita*, *Prithvirajacharita*. It is superfluous to name the various works on poetry, drama, and philosophy, but from the account just given it is sufficient to have an idea of the extraordinary range of subjects dealt with in Samskrit literature, in spite of the fact that much of that literature has been lost owing to the political convulsion that swept over the country.

The volume of Samskrit literature is evident from the consideration of a few typical facts. In 1891 Afrecht published his *Catalogus Catalogorum* enumerating over 30,000 individual Samskrit works. Two later volumes published by him added 10,000 more to the stock, and yet unexplored treasures of Samskrit literature in various places of India still await discovery. Even quite recently some of the countries outside India have yielded their buried treasures of Samskrit literature —*e.g.* the deserts of Gobi and Taklamakan. Even China, Japan, Korea, Tibet, and Mongolia are giving fresh proofs of the extraordinary volume of this literature. The other proof of its vastness is to be found in the fact that in all the principal Samskrit works representative of the principal subjects we have invariably a reference to the works of preceding authors and schools. Panini, for instance, refers to fifteen different schools of grammar that flourished before him ; Kautilya refers to ten different schools ; similarly, Kohala and Vatsayana also refer to various predecessors and schools of thought on the numerous topics dealt with by them.

All this vastness and variety are ultimately due to the extraordinary longevity of the literature ; and even if we date its beginning, with European scholars, from 1500 B.C., it still presents a length of life which is hardly equalled by any other literature of the world. Max Müller, indeed, said that Samskrit literature went to sleep for seven centuries, from the rise of Buddhism in the fourth century B.C. to the rise of the Gupta Empire in the third century A.D., but the results of modern scholarship achieved since the days of Max Müller have proved the falsity of his position. For instance, in the centuries before the Christian era the literary life of the country was represented by such monumental masterpieces as the *Arthasastra* of Kautilya, the *Natyasastra* of Kohala, the dramatic literature of Bhasa, and the *Mahabhashya* of Patanjali. In the centuries immediately following the Christian era we have such famous names as those of Asvaghosha, the renowned guru of the Emperor Kanishka, the celebrated chemist Nagarjuna, the founder of the Mahayana school of Buddhism, together with his illustrious pupils Aryadeva and Maitreyanatha, who all flourished in the interval preceding the Gupta period. In fact, in no period of Indian history do we find any serious interruption of the continuous progress of Samskrit literature, as the result of which we find that it is possessed of an abundance and a variety that are unique in the literatures of the world.

CONCLUSION

Let us now summarise the contributions of Hindu culture to the cause of nationality in India. The foundations of nationality were, as we have already seen, well and truly laid in the very earliest period of our history in the people's possession of a fixed and defined territory, followed by their gradual realisation of it as their common motherland, claiming their homage and service. This realisation was consciously stimulated by an appropriate literature, religious as well as secular, which evoked a widespread feeling of reverence for the country. The country came to be deified, and glorified as being not merely Heaven upon earth, but higher than Heaven itself. But this transfiguration was not a mere attitudinising, or merely due to any play of imagination. The country becomes a spiritual entity because the spiritual enters more into its conception than the material. The country is adored because it is but the embodied type of a living culture. Accordingly, its physical limits were always corresponding with its ideal limits: the country was spreading with the spread of the culture and ideals it stood for. The Vedic river hymn, as we have seen, had its Epic expansion. The original home of the Hindu, limited by the Gangā and the Yamunā in the east, and by the Sarasvatī in the south, extended so as to embrace ultimately the entire continent in successive marches and ever expanding circles. For the country becomes identified with the cultural *environ*, and the ideal country is thus ever carried with the race in its migrations and conquests. It is thus that Brahmāvarta, that "holy land" and original home of the Indo-Aryan between the Sarasvatī and the Drishadvatī (Manu, ii. 17), extends and expands into Brahmarshi-desa (comprising Kurukshetra and the country of the Matsyas, Panchālas, and Surasenakas (*ib.*, 19)), and this again into Madhyadesa (between the Himalayas in the north, the Vindhyas in the south, Prayaga in the east, and Vinascana in the west) and Āryāvarta (lying between these two mountains and extending as far as the eastern and western oceans (*ib.*, 21, 22)), "that land where the black antelope naturally roams." Beyond that lay "the country of the Mlecchas," only to be absorbed in the course of historic evolution in the "holy land," which is continuously spreading until it attains the full limit of its size and stature in the continent of Bhāratavarsha, defined in the Puranas as the whole stretch of space between the Himalayas and the southern seas. The country follows the culture; nay, the culture is one's country and the country one's culture. The soul moulds the body as the body expresses the soul, but the genius of the nation is a vast presence which transcends the actual physical or geographical embodiment, and in its ideal possibilities can indeed embrace the whole world of man. Thus the evolution of India as the mother-country of the Indians has but followed the lines of the cosmic process revealing the Universal in the Particular and the Particular in the Universal. Here is no insular culture lacking in universality, nor a disembodied one which is homeless, and therefore infructuous and sterile.

But this peculiarity has its own effects upon the course of Indian history. Where the country is more a cultural than a material possession, it appeals less to the instinct of appropriation. There is more of disinterested sharing, more of community of life and enjoyment. India thus early became the happy home of many races, cults, and cultures, coexisting in concord, without seeking overlordship or mutual extermination. With this high and complex initial responsibility India becomes the land of composite systems in respect of race, language, civil and personal law, social structure, and religious cult. Other national systems exclude the possibility of such radical diversities, and break down in the attempt to unify them. Federation and Imperialism have perhaps been born too late for their task.

Such composite systems are built up necessarily on the basis of an extended unit of society. Here the social and political composition is based on the group, and not the individual, as the unit : *e.g.* the family, the village community, the caste, and various other similar corporations, of which a special study is made in another work of mine entitled *Local Government in Ancient India* (Clarendon Press, Oxford, 2nd ed., 1920). Such a principle of social construction minimises the friction and collision of atomic units and helps to harmonise the parts in and through the whole. Biologically speaking, such constructions correspond to the more developed forms of organic life which, in their nervous interconnections, show a greater power of integration than the looser and more incoherent organisms lower down in the evolutionary series.

Accordingly, it should be further noted, it is the quasi-instinctive postulates and conventions of group-life which come to be formulated as *law*, and not the mandate, command, or decree of a single, central authority in the State. Law, under these conditions, is not an artifice, but a natural growth of consensus and communal life. Thus ever new social and political constructions arise by the original and direct action of the groups and communities in the State, and not by the intervention of the absolute sovereign power and its creative fiats, as under all centralised constitutions.

The nationality formed on such principles is a composite nationality, and not one of the rigid, unitary type. The relation of the State to its constituent groups becomes, under this scheme, one of copartnership, each maintaining the others in their place. It is not the State that, by its sanction or charter, creates its own constituent bodies or corporations, but, on the other hand, the groups establish, and are established by, the State.

The genius of the Hindus has adhered firmly to this fundamental principle of political organisation amidst the most trying and adverse conditions in the course of their history. Even when the State ceased to be a national or organic one (as under the Mahomedan rule, for instance) they fell back upon the resources and possibilities of that ultimate political creed to work out the necessary adjustments and adaptations to the new situation as means of their self-preservation as a people. They clung fast to their time-honoured and confirmed conception of the State, which was based upon a respect for the original and primary rights of group-life, for the sanctity of natural groupings, the inviolability of the vital modes of human association, to which a full scope was, accordingly, never denied. And thus the Hindu State came naturally to be associated, and indeed very largely identified, with a multitude of institutions and corporations of diverse types, structures, and functions, in and through which the many-sided genius of the race expressed itself. It was these intermediate bodies between the individual and the State which mattered most to the life of the people, to the conservation of their culture, as the real seats and centres of national activity. Accordingly, when a State of this complex composition and structure happens to pass under foreign control, the nation can maintain the freedom of its life and culture by means of that larger and more vital part of the State which is not amenable to foreign control, and is, by design, independent of the central authority. An elaborately devised machinery of social and economic self-government amply safeguards the interests of national life and culture. What is lost is but an inferior and insignificant limb of the body politic: its more vital organs are quite intact. It is as if the mere outwork has fallen:

the main stronghold of national life stands firm and entire against the onslaughts of alien aggression, protected by a deep and wide gulf of separation and aloofness from the domain of central authority, which can find no points of substantial contact with the life of the people and no means of controlling the institutions expressing and moulding that life. It is thus that Hindu culture has had a continuous history uninterrupted by the foreign domination to which a national culture would otherwise succumb.

A complete exposition of this composite type of nationality and polity, such as stands to the credit of India as her special achievement, must wait for another opportunity and occasion. But, in passing, we may as well broadly indicate the lines of its actual operation, and also of its possibilities as an instrument for the unification of the human race or the federation of man. The principles of the Indian political constructions tend naturally, as a closer analysis will show, to reconcile the conflicting claims and ideals of Nationalism and Internationalism in a stable synthesis towards which the League of Nations is hopelessly striving. The relations obtaining within the State between the central authority and the constituent groups on which depend so largely its internal order and peace, form the plan and pattern of its external relations also. Comparative politics, indeed, point to a kind of correspondence between the principles governing the internal constitution of States and the principles governing their external expansion. The *intra*-State and the *inter*-State relations are fundamentally of the same type. The State that is of a central type, and thus absorbs the original and originating groups in its own unitary life, will also exhibit the same militarist spirit of domination and aggression in its movement of expansion by absorbing other States. Similarly, the expansion or extension of the Indian State will not be a process of absorption by assimilation or extermination of external States, neighbourly or rival, but will be governed by those principles, already referred to, which regulate the internal constitution of the State itself in relation to its constituent groups. Those are the principles of a generous comprehension that broaden the basis of an inter-State convention under which all subject peoples are established in their own conventions and all subject States in their own constitution or customary law.

The problems before the League of Nations, of reconciling the self-determination of individual sovereign States with the interests of the collective brotherhood of all the States, will defy solution under the militarist and unitary principles of political formation such as we meet with in the West, but they are amenable to the other method of comprehension which has been explained as the basic principle of the Indian type of State in both its internal and external relations. It is hoped that the Indian experiment in Nationality which seeks, and is called upon, to unify different ethnic stocks and cultures, different systems of law and cult, different groups and corporations, in an all-embracing and all-comprehensive polity, will be found to be a much-needed guide in our progress towards that "far-off divine event to which the whole creation moves," peace on earth and good-will among men.

PRINTED IN GREAT BRITAIN BY NEILL AND CO., LTD., EDINBURGH.